Praise for Michal Rubin's *Home Visit*

Michal Rubin's *Home Visit* is more than a book of poems-it is a demand, righteous and insistent, that we forge a better world. A daughter of Israel and a fierce critic of it, Rubin's poems linger on the details of Israeli occupation: demolished homes, brutalized old men, water-starved villages. Rubin refuses the easy platitudes, "the chanted words / of well- meaning protesters." Instead, she insists, "Words are steps on hot coals." Take it as a promise: these poems will burn away hypocrisy and willful ignorance. Take it as a warning: these poems will sear your heart.
—Toby Altman, author of *Discipline Park*

Michal Rubin's poems of "awoken brokenness" are full of domestic detail-the smell of caramelizing onions, the sleek paper of a childhood story. Such details conjure a world that has shaped the poet indelibly, her feet "marked with the imprint" of the Israel that she has traversed, that she struggles, still, to call home. In poems of grief and outrage, Rubin refigures home to include the Palestinians who also are "held/by the groove of dismayed land." And so we too must be haunted by the image of a child clutching a pillow beside a demolished house. Rubin's incisive, insistent vision takes up the ironies of history and makes them intimate. We cannot refuse to listen when she inscribes her anguish "in the deafness of here." These searing poems make clear that until we learn to embrace our neighbors, we are all in exile.
—Elizabeth Robinson

There Are Days That I Am Dead

Michal Rubin

Fomite
Burlington, VT

ISBN-13: 978-1-967022-00-7
Library of Congress Control Number: 2025933100

Fomite
58 Peru Street
Burlington, VT 05401
www.fomitepress.com

03/14/2025

Table of Contents

Preface

November 8th, 2024

Day 399

The present collection of poems is a jagged painting portraying my inner world since October 7th, the start of the ongoing war in Gaza. Three hundred ninety nine days later, Israelis are still wrapped in the trauma of October 7th, hostages are still held in captivity. Gaza and its people suffer from the devastating response of Israel to the October 7th massacre, with over 40,000 known dead as a result of continuous bombing. Fear, horror, anger, alienation, and helplessness have propelled me to be fully present with my words, the only way I know not to succumb to the cloud of hopelessness.

This collection is dedicated to all Palestinians and Israelis who continue, relentlessly, to work together toward a just peace.

October 8th, 2023

Day 2

Still

You lie on the ground,
a misshapen form you did not choose.

A fly buzzes by, chasing your neighbor's
scent, your silence cuts the sound

of background booms and sirens.
I am far, you are just a photo

on a screen,
a painting of our capabilities.

I am far,
far from the sounds I imagine

but your stillness quakes inside me,
your silence—a scream

into which my words are swallowed—

you lie on the ground,
forbidden to live.

October 11

Day 5

Conversation with my niece, near the Gaza Strip

I roam inside the gloom
the perfume of bombs looms
above the empty tombs a blitz bitts
and bits shards knit the shrouds soon
they will be filled

the tombs

she   said   this   mood   no   longer   suits
her   that   beheading   burning   raping   healed   her   from
compassion   that   babies   on   fire   and   cut   off   breasts   tossed   in
the air reduced her taste for progressive marches

They won

liberation and revenge entwine she said mercy is for fairytales
that limbless bodies wrote another story that poems must be
 bloody to be true she said the silence had awoken her from
slumber and sent her into the fire of revenge

I roam inside the gloom

she said she did not care about criminal courts or my poems
or some conscientious op eds of enlightened thinkers she was
done with understanding or curiosity for motives, you know,
she said she wants them dead   beheading does this to a
person

I roam inside the gloom

4

I tasted her bitter sprayed spit it was warm and soothing and
for a moment it lured me into its welcoming arms it choked
my compassion it birthed my coldness stony cold, I know,
beheading does this to a person

They won

I return to the gloom the perfume
of bombs still looms above the tombs
a blitz bits and bitts shards knit the
shrouds they are filled

the tombs

"I build the kingdom of crying
You vibrate in memory's bow"

Ali Abukhattab

Below the crying
there is a whimper
I search for

           in the wreckage

while I clutch to
my shame
covered with

           colors of war

I move slowly through the aisle
between the rubble
of our worlds

           feeling the vibrating

whimper, all that's left from
the song we come from

October 12

Day 6

Tired

Bless their hearts,

I mutter and stuff my judgements
somewhere
where they can't be found

Have a blessed day,
be with god.

Fourteen hundred Israelis killed in a massacre, women raped and
mutilated, two hundred and forty taken hostages.

What a lovely fall day, it is, thank god

Eleven thousand, eighteen thousand, twenty thousand Palestin-
ians will be killed in Gaza bombing.

I spit the venom
onto the patio floor
it shimmers
a riverbed to southern rain
a bucket filled with pieces
of my foreignness
I touch the sacred cows with my lips
and stare at newspaper photos
from other lands with other
"Bless your hearts"

Welcome back,
So nice to see you,
you were so missed.

Israeli forces dropped white phosphorus bombs on the al-Karama
neighborhood in Gaza.

I stuff another envelope
with wrath and shame
I blurt another
bless their
motherfucking
hearts

tired

of the nice,
of the shimmer of heavy rain on tiles,

tired

of god and
of a far-away old and new war.

"I will never stop howling
I will never stop kicking and cursing
until you come to me…"

Fatena Al Ghorra
Translated by Waleed Al-Bazoon and Naomi Foyle

Your howling I hear in the nights
each howl drips
on me a cigarette burn
marking the days the hours the bodies

I hear your howling
don't stop
I want to know it
to not fear it
to not run

I accept the burns as penance
the howling chases me into the desert
a goat running to Azazel
carrying my sins to the infinite

there I can keen
maybe we both can notice
the screams
in the story
of ancestors

mine and yours

and we can stop the bodies
we can dissent
we can die together
we can tie a ribbon
around the howling
a gift to the gods
maybe they can hear

the ones below don't care

Will there be a day
tomorrow

there is a silence ~~of horror~~
not knowing where to go
whom to talk to
what to say
which words are forbidden
which feelings need to melt
melt with the pain
melt into the day it is
into a tomorrow

and the blue sky of fall

will there be more ~~videos~~
slayed babies in their cribs
posts of the raped
~~last~~ words broken
will there be a day

after tomorrow

and the blue sky of fall

swastikas or celebrations ~~of atrocities~~
celebrations
heinous acts
as if they are liberating

will tomorrow be
trail of tears
of the homeless
between the bleeding ground
and the blue sky of fall

the fall of the fallen ~~hopes~~
the fall of all falls

October 20th

Day 14

The Song I Wish I Had Known

1.
One tear splattered
onto ground
that belonged to someone
we banished

it soaked into their song
and the land drank it

flowers bloomed
a new song.

I speak to the tears
"Go, join your sisters from long ago,
bring back the old song,
for its home is here."

2.
I want to sing it
a keening
above the graves that are marked
above the ones with no stones to mark them
keening

the names on the stones
keening
the missing stones
keening
the dead flowers

On October 20th, Heba Abu Nada, a Palestinian poet and novelist, was
killed by an Israeli airstrike on her home in Khan Younes, Gaza.

New Republic

1.

> *I grant you refuge*
> *from hurt and suffering.*
> —Hiba Abu Nada, (trans. Huda Fakhreddine)

We lived in the second century
of world wars inside seas

I drowned with you
and we sank to the bottom

of the sea of salt
where drowning is not possible

2.

> *You were first created out of love,*
> *so carry nothing but love.*
> —Hiba Abu Nada, (trans. Huda Fakhreddine)

We carried nothing
but each other, in the deep sand

we built another castle
share its floors and words

braided melancholy tunes
into unseen ceilings

3.

> *O! How alone we are!*
> —Hiba Abu Nada, (trans. Huda Fakhreddine)

You and I painted the shadows
we brought along

gave them colors
hung them on the walls of water

to be washed off
in the third century.

.

November 15th

Day 40

In a Field, a Beetle

crawling on a thorn field
the beetle's legs were gripping
the wrinkled uniform of the dead

where swords are clashing
and the present is
the counting of corpses

that's what it looks like
somewhere in the narrow
strip of land

***

I drink Bigelow Sweet Dreams tea
to smooth the image of truth
into the distance

oblivious to the stench of hate
beetle scours the pockets
of the dead uniform

a memorial to the futility
of laughter and the swing set
in the back yard

I pledge empty words

Can you hear
my calling to the fathers
who carry the bodies of
sons

while sending their
second ones for
vengeance

I hold dead flowers
remnants of yesterday's funeral
I lay them on the freshly dug grave
I hand the tissue
to the crying angels

no one sees

I pledge empty words
to the limp body
resting with the relief of endings

they fall on the mound of earth

soaked by the silence

November 15th 2023

Casualties:

Capt. Asaf Master, 22, of Kibbutz Bahan—
Platoon Commander
Capt. Kfir Itzhak Franco, 22, of Jerusalem—
Platoon Commander

https://www.gov.il/en/pages/swords-of-iron-idf-casualties#NO-
VEMBER%202023

At least 11,078 Palestinians have been killed in the Israeli
bombardment of Gaza since October 7. No names are listed.

https://www.aljazeera.com/news/2023/11/15/israel-hamas-
war-list-of-key-events-day-40

"...I am not ready for your wounds and your truths.
you come back to me like a consolation."

Sara Saleh

I am

            waiting in the church of silence

not

            opening my history book

ready

            to call out the lies

for your

            stories look me in the eyes

wounds

            crawl on my body

and your

            your gifts to me are

truths

            jagged unwrapped strewn

you

            and I gather the pieces of them

come

            in a chorus of lamentations

back

            where it all started and you say

to me

            can you birth my howls

like

            they are yours maybe

a consolation

December 5th

Day 60

I held my protest in my hand

It danced,
no, it marched,
on the sidewalks,
in the clouds,
it rose, it sank,
it became dust,
it darkened like ashes
scattered on mountaintops,
in the seas,
on the land
it was heard,
it was unheard,
it appeared,
dis-appeared,
I sang it, I felt it,
it breathed,
my protest, my cry,
my lament, my rage,
there,
it landed
somewhere
no-where

and I held my protest in my hand,
it dripped through my fingers
its heartbeat dimmed

I held its wilted shadow.

I hear them call me a traitor

They call out
piercing the page

traitor

the word lands
somewhere, the place
where my truth happens
where our sins are painted

traitor

I hold the 'traitor' word tightly
I pick up the pierced page
caress its wounds
coax my choked truth
to emerge

It peeks out of its sheltered room
hesitating
yet craving for air
inhaling and exhaling

They call out

Traitor

"This place is all we
ever grieve for - in blurred dreams..."

Deema K. Shehabi

2.

Maybe I have nothing to say. *Sit* I say to myself.
Sit with her anguish. Her grief. Her dreams. Be. Quiet.

Crawl beneath the blurry visions. Enter them.
Dream with her, walk inside the graveyard of her

story. Touch the words in the poem this place
had written. This place you know and don't

know. Walk the streets of her grief, ask for their
name. She tells me about the kid who lived

next door. She paints the rubber bullet embedded
in his eye. I know to stay quiet.

1.

I sat with your quote and my arrogance. I am a therapist.
After all. I can hold one's pain and anger. The denial

has passed. The land was taken. Gone. The pile of broken
furniture amidst the heap of rubble litters my ignorance.

I sat with your quote, bounced it from hand to hand.
I am a therapist. After all. I looked it in the eye, expected

the grief to be mellowed by my gaze, by my expression
of understanding. Let's talk, I said to the quote.

The quote stared back. It's been sitting for days.
For years. Awaiting.

December 6th

Day 61

Prominent Gaza professor and writer, Refaat Alareer, was killed in an airstrike, weeks after telling CNN he and his family had 'nowhere else to go'.

https://www.cnn.com/2023/12/11/middleeast/refaat-alareer-gaza-professor-killed-in-airstrike-intl/index.html

"I am you.
I am your past
And killing me,
You kill you."

Refaat Alareer

We enter the hall of death
we lay on the same soil
damp with the memories

                      yours

mine

the doors slam behind
we abandon living
we engage in the life of death

                      mine

yours

we wander through our stories
projected on the mirrored walls
we touch the etched details in

                      my story

your story

our fingers get lost
where the wind blew
our remains

yours rained

                      on mine

mine

                      colored yours

together we dissolve—
our eulogy
another war

December 15th

Day 70

> "Silence is death, and you, if you talk, you die, and if you
> remain silent, you die. So, speak out and die."
> — Tahar Djaout

On Tuesday god said twice "It is good"

That's why I chose to die on Tuesday. In public. Not just any public, but the kind I hoped would get it. It. The dying, the shedding of a gown of stories. Get it. The nudity of death. Get the craters and folds, the map of a childhood, of moral fairytales dissolving into an afterlife.

I figured god saying "it is good" twice could balance the pockmarks on my skin, each exposing another unvarnished fact. I figured these people are believers, so they can welcome my bald truth. I watched them as each layer was sloshed off, drenching the feet of the curious.

I watched the silence rise. A heavy cloud. Rain was about to dissolve the remnants of my layers. I watched their bodies move. Yearning to break the thickness of death. They watched the bits of stories that breathed in me, lifeless, drowning in the dismantled life.

I heard the eulogy for the dead dream. For the broken sidewalks that were home. For the unmarred falafel smell. For the audacity of presumed safety. For the simplicity of hats in the summer. Each a crumbled layer dropped soundlessly, leaving me behind, in public, naked.

Dec 15 -Washington/Philadelphia, (Reuters) - A Jewish group demanding a ceasefire in Israel's war in Gaza held protests on Thursday in eight U.S. cities on the eighth night of Hanukkah.

https://www.reuters.com/world/us/us-jewish-group-protests-eight-cities-gaza-ceasefire-2023-12-15/

Dec 18 - Thousands have protested in Tel Aviv after Israeli forces killed three Israeli captives waving whiteflags in Gaza.

https://www.aljazeera.com/news/2023/12/18/israel-hamas-war-list-of-key-events-day-73

December 18th

Day 73

In My Sleep

I know you look at me with blindness in my sleep,
I eat some apples falling from the sky, in my sleep

I search for my own eyes.

They have fallen between cracks or got buried
in overgrown grass, rolled on dry earth
beneath my torn sandals.

In my sleep I immerse in silence, lose my hearing,
deaf to the pounding on the door, they come
to get you or me or the neighbor

in my sleep. My lips kiss the emptiness of grief,
my arms reach a naked wall. In my sleep
moments become days

become years
become centuries of hiding in my sleep

I search for my own eyes.

Unsung

Through an old window thin notes of a lullaby
escape and float onto the waves of the night,

swirl around resting daylilies,
chasing fireflies, then with hesitation

linger above the pond mingle with the rhythmic
croaks before they fade into the distance——

leaving behind the scent of a memory,

fade into the void
in search of the missing notes,
the ones lost between shudders
lost between dreams
lost beneath rubbles,
searching
for where it started
searching
for the guardian of melodies
searching
for the guardian
of the unsung notes.

"One day someone will come
and tell the story I recognize"

Mustafah Abu Sneineh
Translated by Katharine Halls

Do you remember the day you looked me in the eye, you said *this
is not so* and I said *yes but* or *yes and*/so we stared beyond the pupils
of our eyes, we marked the stations where we can land together, a
pasture of a blank page where we told our stories together/

There I noticed you are missing an eyelash on the right side of your
left eye, you blinked and you noticed the scar on my forehead, the
remains of chickenpox that left no scars on you and we crawled on
each other's skin/

We noticed the blemish on your shoulder, the scratch on my knee
and we touched with our fingers the grooves on our foreheads,
measured the depth of the story that created the craters on our
faces/

We mapped each other's tales on our bodies, left the streets
nameless, the history dateless, naked we carried our stories into
the world/

January 5th   2024

Day 91

The Hum of a Corner

"I am standing at the corner where there used to be a street"
                                        — Leonard Cohen

Step by step we pluck off our feathers / the ones we used to fly on our
high horses / dip them in ink / write the false stories / I search in the
rubble of my childhood / the rubble of someone's childhood / all is a
wrapping to the inhumanity hum of humans / step by step we walk
into the trap of hate /

In the corner lights and feet honking / the raid comes and my street,
the one I knew, disappears / faces of demons crowded the crossings /
life becomes a moving target / as in phosphorous bombs / the maps of
my being shattered / in stillness /

January 8th

Day 94

Trauma Informed Poem

Monday, June 5th, 1967

I walked past the parked cars, hummed a tune, from memory,
thought of my grandfather,
he was older than the pine trees on the street.

       The air raid siren surprised me.

I knew the make and model of each car, the words of the song dis-
appeared, my grandfather's image gone, I ran, counting the trees,
the planted mile markers, the bomb shelter still distant.

       The air raid siren startled me.

The door to the blue Opel flew open knocking my school bag out
of my hand, tuneless song-line bounced off my tongue, the sirens
echoed in my body, the mile markers lost inside my panic.

       The air raid siren pierced me.

At night, the musty bomb shelter coated my throat, the lady from
the blue Opel, yelled at me for being careless, her panic found
someone to blame, she inhabited my nightmare.

       The air raid siren nestled in me.

Monday, January 8th, 2024

I find no shelter in the faint shadow of my memory, no comfort in recounting my "trauma," I wish to erase the first four stanzas, as small bodies form mounds,

    dead monuments to erasure.

Eight thousand eight hundred kids, no bomb shelters, no air raid sirens to surprise them, no trees to count, no homes to go to, no requiem to hear—

    the rubble envelops their bodies.

Fields seeded by hate, a new crop of soldiers germinates,
the living are hungry, the wounded resting on hospital crumbled floors, twenty one thousand names forbidden to be listed,

    unlit truth worms into my story.

In her refuged collection

she finds a key,
a bag of candy,
for the road before leaving with

a small suitcase, hinges rusted,
carrier of mementos.

It's laid, the suitcase,
small, stashed with others
all shades of ash

patinaed clasps click and squeak
opening and locking, guardians,

black and white photos
faces dissolve into yellowed backgrounds
stories remembered and forgotten,

on tarped tent floor,
she finds the black comb

runs it through her black hair,
desert sand and memories rain
on the tent's floor

she sweeps them with her small hand,
the sand and her memories.

"Once they started invading us.
Taking our houses and trees, drawing lines,
pushing us into tiny places."

Naomi Shihab Nye

So many stones
burying your story.
I pick one,

it collapses into powdered specks—
words, letters, or punctuation.

The specks darting in the air
like my words,
like my letters,

my attempts to find the right turn
in the thick river of howling.

I am baptized in your pain
or in the truth of your telling,
bathe in the air carrying
the dust of your demolished home,

bathe in the oud notes,
its broken strings—my handcuffs.

"We live in the end in a spherical prison"

Ashraf Fayadh
Translated by Waleed Al-Bazoon and Naomi Foyle

My eyes drift from bar to bar
rusted flakes of oxidized iron hang
on their parent stalk, a speck of hope?

Wish for a possibility
of gardening together
on terraces of holy soil?

As ants we will carry seed after seed
and drop them like retired soldiers
enter their new abode,
a new leaf in the scroll we unravel together.

February 1st

Day 118

Numbers

Mohammed, Wadia,
two brothers
Ala Asous, Hazaa, Rami, Ahmed,
four brothers
six cousins
Rizkallah,
seventh cousin,

one missile,
hundred shards of glass,
one ambulance,
one mass funeral,
one village,
one sleepless night
at Muthalath al-Shuhada

I wish my body moved,
shook the numbers off,
22452600
my passport number,

two,
Yehoshua and Rivka, my grandparents,
two,
Rachel and Mimi, my aunts,
they did not get a number,
no ink wasted on their arms
four
bullets outside one small town
in Poland
five
o'clock,
a huge explosion

two
social workers come to help
six
lost parents
a sleepless night Muthalath al-Shuhada

      Stop reading the news,
I am told

counting
countless
counts,
the many zeroes,
trailing digits,
I am lost
with the numbers

On Jan 20th an Israeli aircraft killed seven young Palestinians in Jenin, after one of them apparently threw an explosive device at an Israeli army jeep – and missed. All seven were from the same extended family and the same village.

https://www.haaretz.com/israel-news/twilight-zone/2024-01-20/ ty-article-magazine/.highlight/one-israeli-missile-seven-palestin- ians-killed-four-of-them-brothers/0000018d-2493-dd75-addd- f6f30b320000

Thank You

1.

I got the package
yesterday,
its wrap torn
but it found its way.

I am not sweet in the dusty hills.
Packaged like the chocolate
I got yesterday
I wish I was sent to you.

I am a package lost
no known address
meandering
in the rubble.

You are waiting for me.
You will be disappointed.
I am not the item I was.
Maybe I need to be returned.

The uniforms weigh heavy,
covers the package you won't receive.
The body under the uniform
took a boy to jail.

Nine years old,
he threw a stone
a small one
he was small too.

I wish I could be packaged
mailed to you
I am small and lost
I no longer know my address

2.

I got your postcard yesterday

A memory worms itself
as your face hangs in the air
a child you were   your image
drowns in the rubble

I trace the idea of your smallness
in the dusty hills
your hands on the body
of a nine-year-old

could you free the boy
trapped in the margins
where compassion fades
and take him home?

in my dream I scrub the weight off
as I wash your uniforms
rinse the heavy dust, mother,
you and the boy like brothers

"...the dead can only respond late: 'It's the right of all victims to defend their screams.'"

Mahmoud Darwish
Translated by Josh Calvo

There are days that I am dead.
Without screams. Silently dead. All the screams are locked. A small prison nestles inside my body. They are safe. The screams. They grow old, in their prison. They wilt, become feeble and hoarse.

There are days that I am dead.
I become a cemetery. A field of headstones. I water flower beds. Roots are embroidered around the buried howling. Colors mask the silence. Visitors lay small pebbles. Reminders. Faded names have no voice.

There are days that I am dead.
You visit. I offer apple tea. You sit. I sit. My scream stranded in the shadow of yours. You unfold your poem. Lay it on my headstone. I unfold my poem. Lay it on yours.

"...And remember crimes sometimes
Immortalize their victims
Other times the victimizer"

Fady Joudah

You come in the morning gray cloud
to awaken me

I wrap my sins with your Kafia
send it up to live with the gods

yours we wrap with my grandfather's tallit
and watch it rise into the gray sky

with your fingers you touch the forearm of my people
your trace the inked digits

we call out the numbers together
our etched traumas glow in the hollow space

which we fill with the stories no one wants to hear.

February 18th

Day 135

I left behind the nameless authors' bodies

Seeking refuge from earth
where the tree of knowledge died
I walked into the moon

stripped [off] the uniform
words that lied

oozing blisters

rubbing against the craters

filled with

23,968 stories
24,576 stories
25,733 stories

"Spoke to the birds about it
They told me 'do what we always do
Fly to another place
Then come back with a fresh start
To the same place that you started' "

Farid Bitar

1.

We lie with the limbs of stories,
broken bodies we collected,
numbered.

We flew between the many skies.
We met and made a pact.

Mixed our blood   drops
morphed into purple hearts
we wore on our bosoms.

With urgency we fed each other
from full breasts

and moved in rhythm with silent music
we all heard inside us.

2.

You and I become obsolete
as spring masks the burial of old

questions

new ones will hatch
a resurrection or an exodus,
and there is nothing,

nothing in the books about
the children—
the ones that left their home

carrying a bag with
a pair of underwear.

February 20th

Day 137

On the Fence

I sit on the fence.
I watch.
Sometimes with a moan.

A tall, wide fence.
I sit with comfort.

                    On the fence.
                    Alive.

I watch the bombs
and bullets dance inside,
hint of dusty smoke lands
on my clothes,

                    on the fence.

It clouds my tears,
it clouds my thoughts.

I look at the edges of truth,
the edges of justice,
the edges of prayers,
holding my guilt as a treasure,

                    a trophy,

which I display
and write a short poem about.

I remember to feel guilt,
to make sure the shame colors
the walls of the fence.
I watch the dead buried,
the unfound stories abandoned,
concrete heaps become art,

                                  I sit on the fence.

I notice the fuzzy air,
dust blurs the photos I take
while I feel guilt and shame,
and proud of feeling it.

                                  I notice that I am not the one

                                  dead.

Guernica,   prestigious   magazine,
                    in turmoil
publishing —retracting coexistence
war in the Middle East
                    Israeli writer,
Guernica's webpage   a note,
                    "admin" stating:
"Guernica regrets having published
this piece, and has retracted it..."

https://www.nytimes.com/2024/03/12/arts/
guernica-magazine-staff-quits-israel.html

March 15th

Day 161

"Only when Israelis disassociate from the settler-colonial, apartheid, and genocidal regime and affirm the inalienable rights of those living under Israeli occupation can they begin to engage with Palestinians on the liberation of all..."
—*April Zhu, from resignation letter as a senior editor,*
Guernica Magazine.

Dear April,
I am the colonialist
denier of rights
standing in the town square
fuel-soaked clothes
I am in flames,
my back whipped
I bang my chest
cry of guilt, and
you chant

> *From the river to the sea, Palestine will be free!*

So I sail with the bucket
blood in tow
gold teeth in my pockets
for safe passage,
in the town square
you say fire is not enough,
you sink the ship,

Dear April,
I can't colonize the sea
I float, I cry again
chatati—I have sinned!
I know it's not loud enough,
I row,

46

I float,
I mend words,
I tear my passport pages,
I try to reach some land,
no land, no land,
voices call me a traitor,
voices call me apartheid,
voices reject my fear,
my mother's tombstone,
my grandparents mass grave,

Dear April,
Let me lay down,
surrender,
I will spread my legs,
the lips of my vagina
accept the rape,
an atonement, my breasts
I will give you,
toss them in the air—
a trophy for your
conscientious self—
an offer I make, in the city square,
from within the flames,
or as I drown, leaving
the sea calm as it closes above me,
or the earth smooth, as I am buried
in the drenched soil

Dear April,
is that enough?

March 18th

31,645 + killed and at least 73,676 wounded in the Gaza Strip.

435+ Palestinians killed in the occupied West Bank and East Jerusalem.

October 7th death toll is 1,147.

591 Israeli soldiers killed since October 7, and at least 3,221 injured.

https://mondoweiss.net/2024/03/operation-al-aqsa-flood-day-163-top-eu-official-says-israel-failed-to-prove-its-accusations-against-unrwa/

April 16th

Day 193

At least 60 homes attacked,
some burnt.
Over 100 vehicles burnt.
Dozens of businesses and infrastructures damaged.
Hundreds of animals
slaughtered.

The above events occurred in the villages:
Duma,
al-Mughayir,
A-Sawiya,
Qusrah,
Beitin,
Silwad,
Sinjil,
Beit Furik,
Turmusaya,
Beitillu,
Deir Dobwan,
Aqraba,
Burqin, and
She'b El-Butom

https://x.com/Yesh_Din/status/
1780202961391489322

April 24th

Day 201

The Visit   or   **On Passover**

1.

Death did not pass over us. Year after year from utero on up
we own that moment of the passing over, breathe a sigh
of relief, *death — not upon us this time,* imagining our
doorposts still marked with blood waving death away.
Not this year.

We sing the story, lift the matzah, this year feeling justified,
we eat the bread of affliction, ravage the food, we step out
into the streets, ours, not ours, we pass over, we run over, we trample
over, we stomp over,

we over take, we enter homes of the afflicted at midnight
with roars, we grab a child, a father, topple chairs and tables, leave
the afflicted childless, fatherless, we march in the empty night streets
with pharaoh's hunger we shatter windows shoot some bullets find a tar-
get.

There was no rain in Egypt, nor in the narrow straits we create for others,
the drought dances with the wind knowing, we humans, *the light to other
nations,* are capable of passing over, squashing the afflicted while god is
wondering *what happened to the light* as days darkened under our shadow.

Death does visit, unnoticeably, in silence, it brings no song nor a belated
wisdom. Traces of ashes carried in its coat, shards of window-glass dim-
ming on our table, small memorials to the burnt homes in the village of
Duma, in Beitin, in Silwad, in Sinjil, in Beit Furik...

2.

And then she comes

I didn't expect her to visit. Who am I for her to just show up? Still loaded with food, the table appeared to be smiling as she just walked in, her entourage invisible
was there an entourage?
There was still plenty of food, the table still smiling when I offered a chair, a plate, yes, a red napkin. She sat
or did she?

I didn't know that god sits. Kind of a strange idea. And eats. She did. God ate the chicken I made for Passover.

God refused the gefilte fish. I asked, strangely, because how do you ask god why she came, but I did ask. She said she just heard my poem, she saw the light in the window. She was, she said, confused.
God confused?

Why did I mention her in my poem, she asked. She seemed interested in the orange chicken, as if it is normal for god to just sit and eat, but insisted "Why did you mention me?" a formidable tone in spite of the chicken.

I had to tell her I used her as a prop, an idea in the poem, not real, because she is not real.   She was holding the chicken bone.   I remembered my father would not let us use our fingers to eat chicken, and here she is —no wonder he did not believe. In it.

I had to tell her that she is what my father did not believe. She smiled, she knew, and I started crying because I missed my father and she was not helping. She said it was not her fault, that we are dark, a shadow.

She wiped the ashen remains from the burnt homes off the white table-cloth. "This is not me" she said, looking at her hands, blackened, and had nothing more to say. Nothing.

What did they see in her, I wondered. She has nothing to say—she is

a prop
for my poem
a prop
for the bullets
a prop
for the graffiti
a prop
for demolitions
a prop

God asked for some wine, "The day was difficult" she said "Being a prop
is hard" and wearily reached for the dimming shards of glass.

July 19th

The daily brief

Counting backwards. Day 318 of a war.
Yesterday the yard flooded,
an email hollered at me-
"317 days of slaughter".
I apologize.

Counting backwards. Day 303 of a war.
Ishaq starved to death. His motorcycle
remained under the rubble,
he loved it. The motorcycle. He didn't holler.
I apologize.

Counting backwards. Day 300 of a war.
West of the city, carrying food on his
bike, Khaled rode too close
to the missile. Burial site unknown.
I apologize.

.
●
●
●
●
●
●
●
:
:

Counting backwards. Day 36 of a war.
I am at a conference. Unseasonably warm.
I brought the wrong clothes. Elham
dropped the embroidered bag when
a sniper's bullet reached her.
I apologize.

Counting backwards. Day 13 of a war.
In a poem Hiba wrote *"We are not just
transients passing"*. Her poems rippled
through the world. She was killed.

At home. An airstrike.
I apologize.

In a beginning. Day 1 of this war.
Clear sky, a small pond,
a gentle fall in SC. Horror
surges afar. No flutter in this pond.
I call home.
I don't apologize yet.

They are born through the lines, the words

You speak

I stop to breathe.
The dream of believing emerges
from cracks between the bricks.

I sort with my fingers
splatter of being
a few drops spill,

disappear reappear
in the mist
of colorless clouds.

I am here through the morning
not sure what comes next.

"Inside me a fierce loyalty, the wild thyme of my country,
the flame of pomegranate blossoms, Galilean and sparkling."

Marwan Makhoul
Translated by Raphael Cohen

At night we lie near, kin,
share a murmur of longing,
the lull of dull pain,

the Zatar balm
mists blended breaths,
smooths furrowed brows.

I touch your loyalty with the brown of my eyes
its flavor borrowed
from pomegranate seeds,
sweet and tart, aching comfort.

I don't know yet

I don't know yet about sharing
the land. Maybe a meal, a story,
hold up old photos,
your grandparents, mine.

I can unbury your story,
place it beneath the grapevine,
will you read mine?

You can mark the sidewalk with your feet,
we give a new name for our town,
and our sheep surround us
with the chorus of bleats
remind us of the weeping
we have not yet done.

"Maybe if not one of us falls
We will all rise
Above this hell"

Maya Abu Al Hayat
Translated by Maya Abu Al Hayat and Naomi Foyle

And what if we smooth the wrinkles of the land
can we pick up the fallen

return to the before time
when Jacob met Esau with gifts

pretend that Yitzchak and Yishmael
ran away together

huddled around the fire
in the winter of the desert

can we pick up the fallen
if we smooth the wrinkles of the land?

Acknowledgements

I am deeply grateful to Toby Altman, Elizabeth Robinson, and my writing friends who saw me through my writing and understood the depth of my struggle. My deep gratitude, always, is beyond words for the constant presence and support of my husband, David Reisman.

Thanks to the editors of the following journals for publishing these poems:

"There are days that I am dead"
Cathexis Northwest Press

"Still", "So many stones", "New Republic"
Critical Muslim

"[We enter the hall of death]
Culture Matters

"The Hum of a Corner"
Dissident voice

"Will there be a day tomorrow"
Professing Education

"I left behind the nameless authors' bodies",
"The daily brief"
The New Verse News

"On the Fence", "In her refuged collection"
The Write Launch

"Numbers"
Writers Resist

About the Author

Michal Rubin was born and raised in Israel and has been living in Columbia, SC for the past 33 years, working as a psychotherapist and a cantor. The impetus for her writing is the unending and progressively worsening Israeli-Palestinian conflict. Her poetry wrestles with a mingling attachment to Israel, her birth place, her pain and rage over the years of Israeli oppression of Palestinians, the occupation, and the war in Gaza. She lives with the complexity of having grandparents who were murdered in the Holocaust, and being a member of a "tribe" that practices apartheid.

Her poetry has been published in *Wrath Bearing Tree Journal, Rise Up Journal, Topical Poetry, Full-Lines, The Last Stanza Poetry Journal, Waxing & Waning: A Literary Journal, Palestine-Israel Journal, The New Verse News, Writers Resist, Dissident Voice, Writers Launch*, and *Critical Muslims*. Her chapbook, *Home Visit*, was published by Cathexis Northwest Press in 2024. Her full manuscript, *And the Bones Stay Dry* is forthcoming in early 2025.

Made in the USA
Columbia, SC
30 March 2025

55885341R00043